MINIMS

MINIMS

D. Norel Thims

CANONYMOUS PRESS

IN MEMORIAM

Clara Jeane Haner
[1930—1984]

Linsford Kent Sandven
[1958—1985]

MINIMS

I

maximus

II

major

III

minor

IV

minimus

Fat Porcpise Bauds,
the Mermaids too of Honour,
The Minim Pages,
all the twinkling Host So fill'd,
the Snare of Hell must crack to hold you.
—*Massacre of Paris*

I

maximus

A Mental Inconvenience

Rain brings me inside
pouring me a coffee
to heal the wet sleeve
of short protection
Why isn't memory
committed to me
I seem to recall
remembering the lightning
of a poem, "A"
a heavy poem
in parts, a daily
fugue of twenty-four
pieces, timepieces
timed to release,
alarming me to the fact
that I have no umbrella
to catch the rainwater
washing ashore
on that horizon
sinking under the sun

On Water Walking

Majestic horse walking on water
needs not be led. At will
she drinks, drinks images
liquid images of mirth.
Walking,
walking,
on water
walking.
Never a shore
to pour over
—only water.
Walking,
walking,
on water walking
a horse majestic,
walking,
on water walking.

Eclipse

for my eyes
there is no choice
about the moon,
the way it cuts
the sky,
crowding infinity
out of the picture
and posing itself
as another world

The Horror

I have a horror of it.

It's horrible
to abandon all hope
to burst into tears
to have a weakness for someone
to take a liking to someone
to have confidence in someone
to be in love with someone
to love someone passionately
to long for someone

I'm looking forward to it.

Exclamation Pointless Outside the Temple

Exploited
>> at last
>>>> on a burning barn stage

Cross Mountain's
>>>> uniformed
>>>>>> weathercocks vain
Rivet
>>> themselves
>>>>> to the unseemly sage:
Punk tinder
>>>> immolating
>>>>>> the foiled profane

Bangladesh

Burning destitute runway tarmac
excites the boys when the big bird
flops down: Sex surfaces as the topic
of the hour—why not, it's damn hot
on the burning runway Dacca

Asphalt

Abandoned, set loose
at the side of the road
for a migrant can-picker
itinerant monkey
or peregrine Falcon,
another free verse
bakes in the sun.

Blue Chevy Kept Him Warm at Night

Returning on foot to the place where he ran off
the road he realized the curve was a hairpin
and his tires were bald

Flagging down help he was ignored for hours
in a row until a bicyclist missing two limbs
stopped to ask the way

He pulled Atlas out of his pocket and pointed
magnetic north

Thank you said Handless
Thank you very much

You're welcome but do you perchance
have a match

Identifying Blemishes

Birthmarks,
the fireworks
that linger too long

White caps
on blackheads,
undulations you see

Four-barrelled
carbuncles,
inflamers of combustion

Moles digging
freckled shoals,
pleasing themselves

Scars sharp
Scars blunt
Scars in between

Artifacts all,
dead
on the living

8-5-85

between the borders of midnight
I was expending a personal holiday
on the Istanbul Express through
Yugoslavia   I drank BIPs against
the heat while they lasted
and reviled certain other facts to no end

Carnage in Context

Bloodshed is the general
term for the spilling of blood,
for killing.
Massacre names the promiscuous
killing in great numbers
of those who are defenseless
or helpless to resist.
Slaughter suggests the ruthless
killing on a large scale
of either men or animals.
Carnage suggests the result
of bloody and extensive slaughter,
chiefly of men,
and connotes heaps of corpses.
Slaughter and carnage may be used
of a fair struggle.
Butchery is the savage
taking of human life
as if men were animals.
Havoc is the furious destruction
of life or property,
with panic and confusion,
or of plans and hopes,
as the war played havoc
with his education.

Fetch a Proctor, Someone

Shh! Hackneyed pupils,
  farce-seeing spies,
Constrict the canal
  —resurrect the banal
Retention span, sucking
  carp: undertold stoned
Proclivities, whaling
  —far out, unhinged,
On seas that are crying:
  someone, please

Sub Rosa

They live off subplots in suburbia's subdistricts and subdivisions; they drive subcompacts, Suburu's, or as a substitute they take the subway; they watch films with subtitles; they have names with subtitles; they play subpar golf; they are good at subroutines; they submit to time; they subscribe to subjugation; they speak standard subspeech; they are subconscious and subtle; they are a subspecies subsumed; they are the subculture: they are subversive

Yellow Journalism in *Konkret*

A politicking firebrand
about to be wet
behind the ears
in rhetoric
wags his finger
and his tongue:

    Is this state
    our state?

When canine spray,
a statement incontinent
but true, paints
a natural hue
on today's placard
unwrapped

This is That

this is that state
that state you wish
was another when
you realize it is not
another and die
alive to the fact
the end is nothing
but another end
or beginning if
you will have it
that way again

II

major

Taut in Captivity

Foreign angels appear before my cellar door.
I bid them to enter and they start to sing.
I start to dance deliberately avoiding their toes.
They wince and hint at leaving.
I say no and they begin with rude questions.
I step on their toes.
They start to dance and I, I sang.

Kids Burmese

Before the breeze
of their plains,
calmly, calmly,
calmly sauntering,
Burmese kids
are not gallivanting,
merely calmly,
calmly sauntering.
With that ease
in their longhees,
calmly, calmly,
calmly sauntering,
Burmese kids
are not found wanting,
merely calmly,
calmly sauntering.

Anna Purna's Sanctuary

This All Fools' Day don't behold
the rhododendron welcome of Colossus.
Red folds carpet the way, lulling
pulling you towards steep sanctuary;
but seeming ever nigh, Anna Purna
stands ever highest. At one stiff blow,
your might lets go—
falling
falling
over the depths of snow,
a mere drop to a raging ice sea.
This Fool's Day turned to night,
in otherworldly wonder.

Blind Date with Ben Nevis

No lark in April this time
—more a lion,
springing on Cambridge,
inciting highbrow antics
on the backs of Trinity:
a young woman with split pants punting;
whilst upland is a temperamental
Gaelic fog, one thousand feet too early
for one so foolish as to be caught
making blind dates with mountains.

Hearsay

Inside I'm anywhere
these walls obtaining
in storms of heresy

By Twos and Threes

A damn good wall is what
America needs, a wall

Where a wall, in Iowa,
that's where

A wall in Iowa around Iowa
That's very well what America
needs, a wall around Iowa

A wall round Iowa and Iowa
round every wall is what
America needs in comparison

Matters of Justice, Truth, and the Poor

I took my oath
                I would
                        enquire,
Distinguish
            carefully
                    between these two:
Imperial Adam
               naked
                   in the dew
(There is not much
               that *I*
                   can do);
A Breton
            returns
               to his birthplace
(The poor man's
            sins
                 are glaring—
Seen black
            against
               the fog and snow)
It
   is
      terrible

What cometh
             here
                 from west to east awending:

(One night
             a score
                       of Erris men,
Standing
           under
                    the fobbed . . .)
A spirit
          seems
                   to pass.
Go
    soul
          the body's guest;
Be
     forewarned
                   you old guise:

The laws of God
                  the laws of man

Settling down
to dirty work
takes a perfect
moment of calm
a blank spell
so the mind
can convince
the soul
it's merely
toil that kills

Torch Job

a sheet just this size
virgin or not
sodden or not
gives great heat
combusted at once
  nine past 4:51
  the void is done

Red Noon

A dozen bridges to burn
before I can give the day
its figure of speech:

I might have worked
harder knowing whipped
cream on strawberries

Space-Malls

Built on blueprints 1000000:1 life-scale,
perfectly caulked and hermetic,
theme malls are swarming in orbit,
the apogee of insolence
—domesticated oblivion
where the senses go delirious
among arrays of aisles unto themselves.

Mindwind

Blasting headlong on a 21-cent shampoo
Essence of Raspberry, having been
told to me,
sold to me,
clings to me.
Mindwind blowing through the turnstyle
whistles pretties to market single file.

The Three Propheteers

Is this mirror occupied?
No, feel free.

That was Lie Number One.
Lies Two and Three must be near.

There, behind their ticker
solemnly sniggering,

beguiling
smiling

too gross to invent why
or even a whiter white lie

Public Restitution at Year's End

Dangling hope,
what's a year, anyway,
but a fifty-two week rope,
sway sway swaying
until cut down,
chopped to the ground,
making way for new public measures;
purer than pleasure,
the rite of restitution
makes flaws clear:
dangle the carrot
—then the stick,
the stick, the stick
up up up until morass drips.
Bloody hell,
make them pay
restitution
on New Year's Day.

Fortune Hunted

As I wondered silently
about headstrong bats
that have clung to my outer
screens about to die
there played an unlikely
duet in the background.
A percussive electric cello
intoned on the radio
in sync with delightful burblings
radiating from the winter
pipes. Outside sleet glazed
the night, taking another
winged-rat, oriental symbol
of fortune

III

minor

Silence at Length

I have never known
a Poet: a Poem
I feel, I think
a play for one

Imitation Rain

The air is filled
with leaden speech
ballons. Shadows
balk and thoughts
fall out, splattering
pedestrian heads.
Some call this
beauty. Some
call this truth.
No one calls the bluff.

The Ventriloquist

Sounds the hollow Muse too noisy
Wooden lies, purloined poesy.

From his belly blasts his bellows,
Grainy lines of coarse falsettos.

Smoldering verse the public hears;
Hot curses roil the puppet tears.

O, Pinnochio Purblind Poet,
Would a truer nose dare pare it?

To Talk Nineteen to the Dozen

It's only a manner of speaking
—He didn't mention a word about it
Never to be at a loss for an answer
—You're telling me
You might have told me
—Repeat it, please
I have nothing to add
—Between you and me
I'll be quite frank with you
—Not to mince words
To give someone a piece of one's mind
—I'll take you up on that
I set no great hopes on it
—There's no denying it
Don't let's quarrel about it

Liar

The Day's Great Prevaricator
sits, sedately enthroned
in his electric rocking chair,
fumbling with his mouth organ,
as though to spit—he twits,
and psychophants race to take dictation
from the waste, around, a wheeze
a wheeze: God bless you, King!
What now? is whispered, is answered
Ehh? Ehhh? Nothing, King, nothing
Of course, go on, yes, spittle
dribbles like tears—how touching
now the switch is thrown
the circuit shorted
                    his face contorted

Revel without a Cause

What better
Clan cry
Than this?
To motivate
The masses,
To raise
Them up,
Up off
Their asses,
But better
To unfurl
In curling,
Than undertake
Football clashings,
Where there's
No mind
For every
Head bashing.

In Passing

Boredom overtook me
I hadn't gotten far
I looked in the rearview mirror
It drives a very fast car

The sound of doppler-whining
A honk and then a blur
It left me sitting blindly
Amidst the droning unstirred

Sleep impinges
on my nerves
It has a dream
it wants to tell me
but I won't listen
I'm tired anyway
of naked rehearsals
They lead to greater
rituals and greater
noise despite sleep's
own empty promise

The Juggler's Dream

What it seems is passing this way:
  A Procession of Precession—

     Merry-go-round tag-alongs
     aboard Ferris Wheels
     free-wheeling in time
     with batting clouds
     spinning spatial-8's

Everything suspended—no collision
All animated by gravity's collusion

     Onwards and upwards
     upwards and downwards
     the arch-imperative
     feigning col

         lapse into the past

Quaking, but not

         :awakening

M&M Erotica Eve Dropped

M:
Their active principles
being extremely volatile,
the warmth of the mouth
is sufficient to cause
them to evaporate.

M:
We must not think of sex
at all, but only of the gender
to which these little words apply.

Evening Meal

We ate deeply
stroking the long
tenacious noodles
sucking broth
we a handful
forehead to forehead
eye to eye round
a bowl deep enough
to soothe suspended
feet fired after exertion
famished we slurped
sensuality swelled
sustenance so close
so close sweat mingled
each other's brow
this was the meal

The snake that is my cord
of sound is winding winding
my head with sound sound
inside the snake that is my
sound winding winding sound
inside my head the sound
winding in the snake head
of sound winding snake fakir

/Broken Signal/

I laugh at the rational dream
that smothers me,
and it does me good:
it makes room for the others

high coup de grâce

O drink don't drink drunk
Zenith the feckless adept
runs over peacocks

Four Realized Kernels
of Oriental Wisdom

And it was observed:
    This has no meaning;
And it was observed:
    The meaning is deep;
And it was observed:
    This you cannot understand;
And it was observed:
    The classical is troublesome.

IV

minimus

Black Tea

The smell of tea brewing
makes her sigh, everything
makes her sigh these days
apart from the cottage,
her cottage near the source
of a small valley stream
still pure enough to drink
from, no befoulers or their
ilk within striking distance.
She sighs, raising her tea
to her lips:
too hot it burns
her—she sighs again,
distracted by the pain
of flesh and blood,
the memories of passing
obscenely vivid

Hourglass

Already six years
have yielded
to the quicksands
of time Six years
have funneled
into the gravehole
of dead mother
What a harvest
the grains have been

Dirge

the precocious dead,
exhausted
utterly,
did.
that survives

It is just as well as well as just is it?

The Body Edible

Flay the beast!
Begin the feast!
There are things to make you squirm,
even if you've given up the worm.
Poor nerves?
A few hors-d'œuvres,
sun-tanned,
skin-wrapped,
are no work at all, if
by a humorous apéritif,
you artfully choke them down.
Why the sudden frown?
A salad splashed with intestinal greens,
naughty bits, and hamstring beans
should be just the trick
for those a trifle sick.
Now take delight
(no, it won't bite)
chewing escalloping scapula soup—
very good for the croup.
Yet the Body Edible,
no matter how incredible,
has no main course—
needless-to-say, no recourse
save a new Diet of Worms.

All Over

Crawling again crawling again
crawling crawling crawling

crawl
crawl

crawling again, again
                            again
crawling again

crawling along

        crawling along

                crawling
crawling

crawling crawling
crawling crawling along

crawling
crawling crawling

crawling today
crawling tomorrow

crawling
crawling, but crawling

Creatures of God

if it rains like it rains today
the microfish come to the surface
of the skull, latch onto hair
and lick at the drops until sated
once sated they retreat
microfish are an enigma, that is
I do not understand them
though I do not believe they are
parasites, certainly not like
creatures of god

Vu   **Déjà Vu**

parallel

      lies

      intersecting

truths

intersecting

lies

      truth's

      parallel

Parallax Projection

This hidebound construction
looks very good of parchment;
it updates fully automatically,
a bas-relief of fact,
and encompasses the latest
that big bang bachelors
(of Art of Science) throw out:

    a world-view at a glance

It's rare to get a second chance,
but, and so, to get the first:

    a world-view at a glance

blind

        Of   course

                denied

everything

                                    allow

                to

                         again

I

        do

                    as   we

    by

                        each

   in

        the

MAN

          he

I

                      won't

      that

                happen

won't

      that

            again

he

         said

                  skirted

                    other

      dark

Why They Stare

Why am I brush
ing
My teeth I'm starve
ing
To know why they're stare
ing
I'm starve
ing
They are stare
ing
I am starve
ing
I am
ing
I
ing
ing
To know why they stare.

Paper Cuts

Does sagebrush tumble
Brittle old men tumble
veritable ghosts
rolling in veritable ghost towns
taking last looks
Spooks, you might say
looking away

Solomon's Wish

Someone forgot to laugh.
It was Solomon's funeral and someone
forgot to laugh.
It was his wish, this laughing, but someone
forgot.
How could he forget?
But he did.
He wasn't even there, at the funeral.
He knew.
But he forgot to laugh.
The laughing and the funeral were supposed
to go together.
But he forgot.
He forgot to laugh.
The laughing, it was his wish, at the funeral.
The wish was laughing at the funeral.
But he forgot.
The wish was forgotten.
The funeral wasn't.
He remembered the funeral.
But the wish he forgot.
He wasn't at the funeral and he forgot the
wish to laugh.
He wished he had forgotten the funeral.
But it was the wish he forgot.
He forgot to laugh.
It was Solomon's wish to laugh at his
funeral.

And he forgot.
He wasn't even at his funeral.
He forgot to laugh at his funeral, which he
wasn't even at.
How could he do that?
How could he forget to laugh at his funeral?
He forgot his wish.
The wish, the laughing, he forgot.
He forgot to laugh at the funeral.
It was his wish.
He wasn't at the funeral.
He didn't laugh because he forgot.
He didn't forget Solomon.
He didn't forget the funeral.
He didn't forget Solomon's funeral.
But he forgot to laugh, which was
Solomon's wish.
Solomon's wish was to laugh at his funeral.
Someone wasn't at his funeral and someone
forgot.
Someone forgot to laugh.
Someone forgot.
Solomon was someone.
Solomon forgot.
Solomon forgot to laugh.

Here

I do nothing. Words are impotent in the face of the Possum King. Audiences are random, audiences are seldom. I wait. I will wait. I will have waited when I wait no more. This is how it has been. Ought enters not. Facts, and alone facts. The Possum King twitches, but it is false, he stops. He twitches again and again he stops. False stops. Wait. Do nothing. Wait. Twitches are seldom, twitches are false. False. Nothing. To do, random. Wait. Events. False. Events. False. Events. Wait. False. Where is the Possum King, false. Possum King, false. Possum King, wait false. Possum King. Here again.

The Apologist

I'm sorry.
It's perfect.
There was nothing I could do.
I'm perfectly sorry.
It's perfect.
There was nothing I could do.
I'm so sorry, so very sorry.
It's perfect.
There was nothing I could do.
I'm so very, very sorry.
It's perfect.
There was nothing I could do.
Don't be mad, I'm sorry.
It's perfect.
There was nothing I could do.